Holland
in cameracolour

Holland
in cameracolour

Photographs by F. A. H. BLOEMENDAL

Text by MARGARET HIDES

LONDON

IAN ALLAN LTD

First published 1975

ISBN 0 7110 0598 2

© Ian Allan Ltd, 1975

Published by Ian Allan Ltd, Shepperton, Surrey
and printed in Italy by
Graphische Betriebe Athesia, Bolzano

Introduction

'GOD made the world, but the Dutch made Holland' runs a famous Dutch epigram. It is not entirely facetious because without their windmills, dikes, dams and polders the entire north and west of the Netherlands would not exist.

That word polder is commonplace to the Dutch. It is so basic to the history of their country. But a stranger may need a translation: polder means reclaimed land.

So, as the Dutch say, welcome under water.

There are nearly 13 million people living in that state. Moreover, to confound the statisticians, anything written about the size of the country (at present roughly 13,500 square miles, 190 miles long and 120 miles across at its widest) could be out of date by the time you read it. By then the incredible inhabitants will probably have won more from the sea.

Centuries of practice in preventing it from slipping back have made them hardy, intensely practical — so much so that they build cemeteries on artificially constructed hills, about six feet high, to keep the coffins dry. Not surprisingly they have become the world's land reclamation experts.

Holland, often wrongly dismissed or bypassed by people who believe it will be monotonously flat, offers an embarrassment of riches. There are hills and castles; there are cities with bright lights and entertainment set on clean wide waterways; there is a cache of art and a treasurehouse of history which is brought up to date with the gallant story of our own times.

The landscape is never uninteresting. An inland combination of low-lying green meadows and canals is broken not only by windmills and picturesque swing bridges, but by the outline of modern industrial cities, or the tell-tale derricks of an international port, and the masts of fishing boats in some ancient harbour.

Straight, fast motorways dissect this country where no frontier is more than three and a half hours drive from the capital. It is simple, however, to turn aside from the busy main routes and go meandering into interesting villages and off-the-beaten-track towns.

It is inaccurate to use the name Holland when referring to the whole Kingdom of the Netherlands, but it is not easy to discard this generally accepted English usage. North and South Holland are merely two of the country's eleven provinces; they have the seat of government and the greatest concentration of commerce, with The Hague, Amsterdam and Rotterdam among their cities.

North Holland, mostly below sea level, protected by a line of sand dunes and artificial dikes, occupies the great peninsula jutting northwards between the North Sea and the Ijsselmeer (better known as the Zuyder Zee). Some of its lovely old towns are Hoorn, Alkmaar, Edam and Den Helder.

South Holland lies on the western seaboard and has just the appearance travellers expect: a bonus of blond beaches, tulip fields, windmills, canals and vast lakeland expanses.

However, the Netherlands has not been created from the sea alone. The east of the country, and parts of the middle and south, are not below sea level and cannot be inundated. Real hills are found in the south, where the Netherlands meets her neighbours, Belgium and Germany. Limburg, the southernmost province, holds many surprises. Without being imposing or overwhelming it is extremely pleasant. You look in vain for the familiar Dutch landscape of windmills and canals. The skyline is one of tall church steeples seen across unbroken farmlands of wheat and barley, and acres of market garden produce.

There are hills (first gear for a car) and castles (first-class accommodation for the tourist in some). By mid-May the rolling countryside is thick with orchard blossom; by July cherries hang fat and dark red on trees, and strawberries are sold at the roadside.

THERE were settlers in the Netherlands more than 5,000 years before Christ. Archaeologists believe that by 3,000 BC well organised communities thrived on the higher land, safe from the sea, their ships trading with the Baltic and Egypt.

As a united entity it is not an old nation. In the Middle Ages it was no more than a geographical unit divided into autonomous duchies, although several Dutch towns were prosperous trading centres ruled by a merchant oligarchy.

It was part of the Hapsburg Empire in the sixteenth century at a time when the Reformation was sweeping Europe, and through hereditary links with the rulers it had come under Spanish domination when the teachings of Martin Luther, and more especially of Picardy-born John Calvin, found a natural home among the serious-minded Dutch.

Repressively barbaric counter-measures taken by the ruler, the Spanish King Philip II, provoked a national revolt in 1572, led by Prince William of Orange ('William the Silent'). After William's assassination his son Maurice, continuing the struggle, broke Spanish domination by 1609, but not for a further 39 years did Spain acknowledge the fact. The culmination was the independence of a Republic of the seven United Netherlands in 1648. This determined fight of almost eight decades is recorded by historians as 'the longest, bravest and most cruel struggle for freedom in all history.' During those 80 years the centre of world trade had shifted from the south and the Lowlands to the cities of Holland proper.

With a growing reputation as a place of shelter and tolerance, the Netherlands became a haven for refugees. The Pilgrim Fathers, 101 English Puritans, sought asylum from persecution in their own country. After a short period in Amsterdam they moved to Leiden before sending a small advance party, chosen from volunteers among their community, to America in 1620. They sailed from Holland in the *Speedwell*, before embarking for the remainder of their historic journey from England in the *Mayflower*.

Other refugees, from England, France, Spain, Portugal, many of them highly cultured, competent craftsmen and businessmen, brought their considerable skills to a nation of shipbuilders and seamen. The combination proved dynamic. With fleets that were the mightiest on the seven seas, the Netherlands grew prosperous from trade. From Norway came wood, for the piles on which her great cities, spreading from newly reclaimed land, rested. Cocoa was imported from South America; silks and brocades from the East; wines from Spain and France; spices from India; and tobacco from New Amsterdam (later to be lost as a possession and to become New York). This Dutch settlement along the shores of 'New Holland' was the Netherlands' colonial stake in America.

Commerce followed the ships. The Netherlands became leaders in international banking, insurance and trade. Cities, farmers, merchants flourished; the Dutch East Indies Company, and soon afterwards the Dutch West Indies Company, were founded; the Golden Age was well into its glory by the middle of the seventeenth century.

By the end of the century a jealous England and France engaged Holland in war, but in the face of the greater threat from France Holland composed her differences with England, sealing a long-lasting alliance with the marriage in 1677 of William of Orange to Princess Mary, daughter of James II.

In 1672 the Dutch, at great cost to themselves, repelled invading French armies by opening their dikes on Amsterdam. The nation's dikes were never again deliberately breached in the face of an enemy until World War II.

Eighteenth-century inheritors of the Golden Age began to rest on their laurels. Enterprise diminished, continuing strife with France exhausted the North, costly colonisation replaced shipbuilding and astute trading, and at the turn of this century Napoleon was in charge, with his brother Louis king.

After the Congress of Vienna in 1814 William I returned from exile, and Belgium was linked in uneasy union until the Brussels revolt of 1830 led to their separation. In 1840 William abdicated in favour of his son, who had served in the British army at Waterloo. His son in turn reigned from 1849 to 1890, when Wilhelmina, mother of the present Queen Juliana, came to the throne.

6   Neutral in World War I, Holland was invaded by the Nazis on May 10th, 1940. Among the

most gallant sagas of World War II are the extraordinary lengths to which Holland went to save her Jewish population from deportation. The Dutch underground, and many ordinary citizens, risked their lives to hide or to get to safety as many of the 140,000 Jews as they could. They never relaxed in compassion and vigilance throughout the war, and there are many memorials testifying to this, such as the Anne Frank House and the statue to the Amsterdam dock workers who in 1941 fought with bare hands the heavily armed soldiers sent to round up several hundred young Jewish colleagues.

By the end of September, 1944, Allied armies, having liberated France, were ready to sweep into the Low Countries, and some of the war's final, decisive battles were fought in the Netherlands. Queen Wilhelmina, in her autobiography, writes of the dead of Amsterdam being stacked up in the Zuiderkerk when they could no longer be buried.

Since the end of World War II the Netherlands, like other colonial powers, has undergone political and social change. When Japan's wartime occupation of the East Indies ended 40,000 Dutch were freed and returned home, to a country not yet recovered from German occupation. Indonesian independence from the Netherlands in 1949 added an enormous wave of Eurasian families to the kingdom's population, but, led by the Queen, who briefly shared some of her accommodation after welcoming the first immigrants, the Dutch responded to the challenge. They allocated housing on a large scale, squeezed up a bit more and proved yet again that tolerance was not the prerogative of their seventeenth-century ancestors. The antipathy between immigrant populations and nationals which has increasingly beset Europe's ex-colonial countries has touched Holland only mildly in the early 1970s.

The Dutch Government, determined to avoid urban sprawl and pollution in the rest of the 20th Century, even though by the year 2,000 it is envisaged that 18 million people will be living in about 14,000 square miles, passed the National Physical Planning Act in 1965. A national physical planning agency is now based in The Hague and works closely with local authorities blueprinting for a tolerable future.

'A LIVING NATION builds for the future' is the motto carved on the stone monument to the Zuyder Zee engineers.

The Zuyder Zee project, a fifty year reclamation plan, comes to fulfilment at the end of the present decade. It has been one of the greatest engineering achievements of all time, gaining over half a million acres from the sea and shortening the coastline by about 200 miles.

The Dutch have been building dikes for 1,500 years. The first were of earth, constructed with bare hands and primitive tools; then they were of stone; today they are made of steel and concrete. As soon as an area had been walled off it was drained, often by water pumping windmills. This created a *polder*.

The dike already existed in a crude form when the Romans occupied the country south of the Rhine. During the Crusades Hollanders accompanying the eleventh and twelfth century Christian armies performed what were to the people of the Holy Land hydraulic miracles.

In more than half the total area of the Netherlands people live and work below sea level. Schiphol airport, Amsterdam, is 13ft below sea level. The land on which it stands was reclaimed just over a century ago from Lake Haarlem. Old paintings show full-scale battles between Dutch and Spanish ships on the lake. Fifteenth-century charts mark its position as an enormous deep, dangerous lake — 'Schip Hol', literally a hole for ships.

The easiest way for the non-technically-minded traveller to grasp something of the enormity and excitement of the land reclamation story is to tour Flevoland, that vast *polder* area created when the Zuyder Zee was dammed off from the North Sea and renamed the Ijsel Lake, or Ijsselmeer. Flevoland lies only a few miles north-east of Amsterdam. The 7 capital' of the East Flevoland polder, Lelystad, rose from the primæval mud less than ten years ago. You see it lying very low, almost crouching against the horizon as you approach by road.

Dutch families take picnics in Flevoland and sit happily admiring panoramas of the world's most advanced reclamation machinery. But there is undeniable excitement in sitting on the bottom of the Zuyder Zee — or what was until very recently the bottom before they got around to reclaiming that particular section. You see exactly how nature takes over after water has been removed, the first vegetation which fluffs on earth newly exposed. You need to take care not to run over sea birds still unused to traffic. Yachts and commercial water traffic sail on the still undrained sections to complete the awesome juxtaposition of new earth, great machines, new cities, and expansive stretches of water.

City planners set out to create in Lelystad a vital twentieth century city — tree-lined streets, green lawns and open spaces; houses in preference to apartment blocks; submerged highways to free the air of pollution; a central complex of shops; a swimming pool; and a sports ground that children can reach without the hazard of crossing busy roads.

From the small nucleus of families who moved into houses ready built to receive them (with all equipment ultra-modern, down to piped TV from community aerial) in 1967, the population has risen by nearly 5,000. It is expected that it will be a city of 100,000 by the end of this century.

ARCHITECTURE in Holland is amazingly varied. In particular, Delft, small and tidy, presents concentrated, ordered glimpses into the best of Holland's past at every turning. Its streets are narrow, pierced by canals, and its bridges high-arched and ancient. Houses are step-roofed with leaded windows, and ornate patrician doorways, usually with a double row of steps, lead up to double entrance doors. The church is fifteenth century. The Prinsenhof was originally an abbey.

The country has over 300 castles and stately homes, but generally the buildings are small and domestic in character. They range from the seventeenth-century patrician homes of great cities and the ultra-modern of the polder cities to the clapboard houses of North Holland and the characteristic farmhouses of Friesland, with their enormous single roofs and glazed tiling.

One of the unique features of the seventeenth-century houses lining canal banks is the block-and-tackle hoisting beam at roof level, used for hauling furniture and merchandise into houses where the stairs are so steep and narrow that hardly anything can be got up them. The Dutch say you can always tell whether or not a man is a gentleman by the way he treats a lady on these old stairways; if he tries to get behind her, then he is a lecher.

Of major architectural importance are the Romanesque churches of Maastricht and Utrecht. They are not strictly representative, however, because the sandy nature of much of the soil makes massive buildings unsupportable in most of Holland.

Some of the finest cities — Delft, Haarlem, The Hague, Utrecht, Amsterdam — owe much of their beauty to a single generation of boom-time builders in the Golden Age, when the influence of classical Italian and French styles was coupled with the affluence of the Dutch merchants. Many civic buildings of this time are particularly attractive. Influenced by the foreign intellectuals, especially the Flemish, who entered the country, Dutch builders exchanged the rather clumping ornateness and the gabling of earlier, purely Dutch architecture for greater elegance and grace, only to have the eighteenth-century builders run riot with rococo.

Hofjes — houses where elderly people could live independently and in dignity — were built as much as 350 years ago. Some outstanding architectural examples are still in use, and they supplement the modern colonies of old people's apartments and bungalows throughout the country. Many of the old cities have *hofjes*. The visitor to Amsterdam can find some lovely examples, including the Deutzenhof (855-899 Prinsengracht) and the enchanting Begijnhof. Well known and easy to locate, the Begijnhof is perhaps not in the purest sense a *hofje*, but it is regarded as one nowadays, and it is an architecturally exquisite corner of old Amsterdam that no visitor should miss.

The importance and wealth that came to flourishing seaports at the heyday of the Dutch East Indies Company can be seen in the architecture of some of the old trading cities of the Ijsselmeer: Hoorn, where the whole town is practically an architectural museum; Medemblik, with a thirteenth-century castle not far from a modern pumping station; and Enkhuizen, whose Zuider Zee museum is in the walls of the old fortifications. Such places are often wrongly labelled 'dying' cities, but their dreamy quality has not robbed them of vitality.

Post-war planners have turned destruction to good account, with advanced and workable ideas in apartment blocks, housing estates, offices, railway stations, shopping precincts and civic buildings — best seen in cities like Arnhem and Nijmegen, or those growing *polder* cities of the twenty-first century, such as Lelystad.

CITY planning at its modern best can be seen in Rotterdam's reconstructed centre, whether in its underground railway, the acoustically perfect Doelen concert hall, its apartment blocks or the traffic-free shopping precincts with outdoor aviaries and flower beds along the centre of smart shopping avenues. The high-quality goods in the shop windows are evidence of its prosperity.

Rotterdam is a city to make the heart glad, for it supplies one of the answers man has found it possible to make to inhumanity and destruction. On May 14th, 1940, the city sustained almost one third of the total war damage suffered by the Netherlands. The heart was ripped out by Nazi bombers; 900 acres lay in absolute ruin, hundreds of civilians were dead. Four days later the city gvernment began planning the reconstruction.

Today only the complete newness of almost everything betrays much of the story, but the Rotterdammers' reply has gone further than mere replacement. The city has become the largest port in the world and is often jokingly referred to as a port with a city. Its people love the maritime flavour.

Twenty years ago astute gauging of the world's future oil demands and of the colossal size to which transporters would grow made the planners prepare harbour installations, storage facilities and refineries, which have become capable of meeting the needs of practically all Europe in the seventies.

Best way to enjoy the tremendous sea spectacle is from the top-deck-restaurant of the 392ft Euromast, which towers above the panoply of miles of quays and shipping.

Amsterdam, though not the seat of government, is the capital of the Netherlands. A thousand years ago it was a fishing hamlet on the river Amstel. Four hundred years later it grew into a city so brilliantly engineered on wooden piles driven deep into the sea that it has stayed the pace, unlike lovely Venice on her shifting sands, and become an important international port as well as a major European commercial centre and a place of gaiety and entertainment. Today Amsterdam might justly claim to be Europe's avant garde city.

It is tempting to offer only an image of patrician mansions, 40 canals, 400 bridges, ancient churches, elegant shops, and museums filled with famous works of art, but Amsterdam is too much a capital of the latter half of the twentieth century for this to be the complete picture.

There are top-class night clubs, theatres, restaurants, cinemas. The thread of tolerance running through Holland's story is nowhere more evident than in the capital. Dubbed sometimes permissive, sometimes broadminded, sometimes free-and-easy, a haven for the world's flotsam and jetsam, it is here that the establishment and the growing anti-establishment of the decade still face each other with a fair degree of tolerance.

Societies through which the young seek to change everything flourish without harsh repression, often with considerable understanding. They include women's lib, hippies, the legalising of soft drugs, homosexual clubs, anti-pollution demonstrations, a Hara Krishna temple.

The ideal that you live-and-let-live is not new in Amsterdam. Three hundred and fifty years ago the oppressed minorities of Europe doubled her population within 25 years when they fled from intolerance in their own countries. By 1650 half her population was non-Dutch.

From this mixture has sprung the singular individual, the Amsterdammer. He is an individual not to be pushed around, an idividual who prefers things on the surface rather than swept under the carpet.

Amsterdam is a capital not only for all ages but also for all seasons. Seasonal changes do not erase the elegance or the bright lights which exist side by side as in few other world capitals.

Spring is the time when new leaves appear faintly on the trees to etch the clear characteristics of each canal. Spring is a time of gentle transformation in the Jordaan, that enchanting central district equivalent in spirit and camaraderie to London's cockney east end: a maze of tiny streets and canals and narrow leaning houses with hoisting beams, it has quiet squares and some of the best taverns in town. Recent talk of pulling much of it down roused dissenting voices loud and clear from all quarters.

Summer is the season for top flavour strawberries and thick whipped cream; the season for a tourist influx, for hippies sprouting on the Dam, the season for illuminated bridges and buildings, canal rides in glass-topped boats with candlelit suppers, music and wine on board.

Autumn is the time gold and neon — the time for the first tureens of pea soup so thick you can stand a spoon up in it, served (if you ask) with a side plate of meaty ham or oxtail bones.

In winter, the lights from tall uncurtained windows in the old canalside houses shaft between the bare branches on the water, streaking wiggling patterns in orange and yellow across the surface. When snow falls corners of the city can become a Brueghel sprung to life.

There are good places to eat, good taverns in which to drink: go between five and seven in the evening, the time the Dutch call 'the bitter hour', to find the places full of the locals. The carillons of beautiful old churches will mark out your hours all over the city.

Over four thousand seventeenth-century houses, preserved, protected, still in use, add to the elegance. Some are memorials to the city's resistance to intolerance. The Anne Frank house (263 Prinsengracht) is now used as a meeting place for young people of all nationalities. Visit it preferably at the end of a day's sightseeing; its searing impact leaves you deeply moved hours afterwards. There is also a lovely concealed church, 'Our Lord in the Attic' (40 Oudezijds Voorburgwal), relic of the days of Catholic harassment. Close by is the Oude Kerk, the city's oldest church (1306).

The Netherlands form a constitutional monarchy under the house of Orange-Nassau, with two Chambers of the States-General exercising legislative powers and eleven provinces, with various municipal councils, legislating local government. Seat of Parliament, and of the International Court of Justice, is The Hague (also known as Den Haag and Gravenhage). Unlike Amsterdam, the expansion of The Hague was not restricted by a maze of canals; it came into being as an 'open city' after that period when there was need for fortifications and defence moats. While builders expanding many of the great canal cities were forced to build upwards, the noblemen and merchants of The Hague could spread outwards, with fine mansions set amid parkland and tree-lined approaches.

This spread was on a surprisingly modern grid pattern and the city has an ordered, green look. You feel much of the time that you are in a park.

Among its superb buildings there is some particularly fine Renaissance and Gothic architecture. A remarkable group of buildings is enclosed in the Binnenhof, comprising a thirteenth-century 'Hall of Knights', the Upper and Lower Houses of the States-General, adjoining which it the Mauritshuis, set at the side of a lake. The Mauritshuis has become an elegant museum housing a very fine collection of old masters.

The Hague has an attractive seaside suburb, Scheveningen, with good beaches, smart hotels and small guest houses and a charming old inner harbour which somehow manages to keep itself remarkably separate from the sophisticated end of the town.

In complete contrast Maastricht, provincial capital of the south, retains a wealth of bastions and towers from the days of turbulent frontier clashes when it withstood nineteen ferocious sieges. This tail-end of the country in the province of Limburg, where the Netherlands meets neighbouring Belgium and Germany, was already important in Roman times. It is located at an intersection of Europe's great roads and river trading routes. There is no *polderland* here.

During World War II in St Pietersberg Hill on the city perimeter man-made tunnels, a thousand years old, sheltered from an enemy too afraid to penetrate its labyrinths some of the country's great art treasures — Rembrandt's *Night Watch* among them. These amazing geological curiosities, a refuge for many kinds of bats, provided hiding places for Allied servicemen and resistance workers and housed a secret library, hospital, chapel, electrical generator and dormitories sufficient for 9,000 people. All this was done without disturbing the prehistoric fossils and the enormous chalk column autographed since 1307 and bearing the signatures of Napoleon, William of Orange, Sir Walter Scott, Voltaire among others. Tourists are welcome in St Pietersberg Hill today.

Thorn, another of the country's southern gems, has origins going back a thousand years. It aspired to being one of Europe's great bishoprics before apparently falling asleep again. To see it is to step back in time. A main arterial road, cutting it off from anyone who does not know to turn aside and seek it out, hides its elegant old squares, gas-lit cobbled streets and whitewashed houses.

REMBRANDT and Holland are synonymous. On my first visit to Amsterdam I remember asking a man in the street for directions. He stood for a moment, obviously searching for some common denominator which he and a stranger to his city might have. Suddenly he said, "You know the building where is kept Rembrandt's *Night Watch*?" When I nodded he took the Rijksmuseum as my bearing for further instructions.

I think there are few other cities in the world, perhaps only Florence, where you might be directed by a painting. The Dutch, keenly aware of their cultural heritage, visit their museums much as tourists do.

The history of the Netherlands' remarkable wealth of art is long and complicated. The seventeenth century, the period of Rembrandt, Frans Hals and Vermeer, does not have a monopoly of her extraordinary flowering of European art. This was sparked off by the religiously inspired destruction of much of the great Catholic church treasures accrued from the Middle Ages.

The Romanesque of the southern Meuse region — 11th to 13th centuries — which culminated in the architectural glories of Maastricht and Roermond, has left churches and ecclesiastical treasures which are among the finest of the great Rhenish churches in Europe.

Towards the end of the Middle Ages, when the Dukes of Burgundy were attempting to found an empire combining almost all of the Netherlands with important parts of eastern and central France, the late Gothic style spread from Brabant throughout the Netherlands. Nearly all the great Gothic churches in the country were built in the fifteenth and sixteenth centuries, but as the style came northwards it became plainer, much less gilded and ornate. Reclaimed land could not support heavy loads on marshy foundations, so a simple style

11

evolved, wood in the vaults replacing stone; it was often shaped by the builders, experienced seamen and shipbuilders, like the upturned hulls of ships.

Artists contemporary with these times were Van Eyck and Hieronymus Bosch. The meaningful, tense work of Bosch revealed as no painter had done before something of the tremendous crisis of the age — when great European humanists, such as Erasmus and Sir Thomas More, corresponded with each other in the hope of resolving weighty dilemmas.

Then came the classic baroque of the seventeenth century, expressed in the patrician houses of traders, of merchant princes and bankers, the men of Holland's new global commerce, whose hard-won Protestantism forbade flourishing displays of grandeur such as their French contemporary *chateau* builders were creating.

For a time the eighteenth-century violence of Napoleonic wars and the falling apart of an era seemed likely to wipe out inspiration, but by the end of the century a new, gentle humanism came in. Equal rights became important; interest centred on technical problems and physics.

With the second half of the nineteenth century the Hague and Amsterdam schools prompted a revival of Dutch painting, led by such artists as the three Maris brothers, Israels and Vincent van Gogh. The best collection of Van Goghs in the world can be seen at the Stedelijk museum in Amsterdam.

However, Dutch art and creativity do not stop at her museum doors, or with her architecture. There is a long tradition of furniture designing. Dutch pewter, Leerdam glass, Delft tiles and pottery are supremely fine. The development of the carillon has been nurtured here too, and out of more than 100 which remain today over 20 carillons are still of the first importance.

The Government subsidises several of the Netherlands orchestras. The Amsterdam Concertgebouw and The Hague Residentie are internationally famous. A national ballet group and a national opera company tour the country from their Amsterdam bases. Each June and July, during the month-long Holland Festival, artists gather from all over the world to perform before capacity audiences.

The festival is not confined to the capital or the seat of government — or to music and drama. Performances take place in towns all over the country and art galleries put on special exhibitions. The Holland Festival, more than any other comparable international event, is truly a countrywide affair.

THE Netherlands is the centre of the world's diamond cutting and polishing industry. Britain still keeps tight controls on the marketing of diamonds, but the expertise which goes into turning the rough stones into gems of great beauty belongs to the Dutch.

The first rough diamond is said to have been found in India thirty centuries ago, but for Europe the story only seriously begins in 1586 — in the Netherlands. The Amsterdam diamond cutting industry became a tradition, descending from father to son, from uncle to nephew.

In 1727 when the rich diamond fields were found in Brazil an agreement was made at that time that Brazilian diamonds would be sold only in the Netherlands. The city's diamond industry became world-famous. With the nineteenth-century discovery of the first stone in South Africa, it blossomed as never before. The Amsterdam Coster factory was the one entrusted to cut the Koh-i-noor diamond.

Women turned the cutting and polishing wheels. Later (the fore-runner of women's lib?) they were replaced by horses! In the nineteenth century steam engines took over.

You can visit diamond factories in Amsterdam without charge. Holshuijsen-Stoeltie (13 Wagenstraat, near Rembrandtsplein) is one of the many — not the largest but they do take time and trouble, explaining clearly the hard facts and lore of diamonds. Do not expect a dazzling display of gems at a diamond factory. You see mostly overalled men, who are the skilled cutters and polishers, bending over individual benches on which the diamonds are minute specks on the end of special holding tools.

Holland, a highly industrialised country, attracts large amounts of foreign investment. Linked to her age-old penchant for banking, finance and insurance, this makes for business on a worldwide scale.

Nearly half the working population is employed in over 200,000 industrial companies. Oil and chemical plants are paramount in the economy. The Fokker plane is high among her exports; so too is the DAF automatic car and the DAF truck. The electrical giant, Philips of Eindhoven, sending more abroad than to its home customers, ranks as one of the top three in the world's suppliers of radios, television sets, vacuum cleaners, domestic appliances and radar equipment.

With the exception of enormous supplies of natural gas and salt, and some oil and coal, the Netherlands lacks many raw materials, so that she imports much more than she exports. But the deficit is made up in shipbuilding, bridge building, transport of goods by sea, and the storage of large quantities of oil, grain and foodstuffs, as well as by large revenues from the international supervision of water engineering projects.

No description of Holland's economy is complete without some account of the bulb industry. Millions of flower bulbs leave Holland each year. Behind their growth and their packing, shipping and air freighting is a Flower Bulb Research Laboratory with a great deal of government money as well as private enterprise finance and a lot of no-nonsense disease control

To see the best of the bulbs — a public relations image of Holland to the tourist but a £50 millions a years export industry to the businesslike Dutch — go in April/May and tour an area bounded by an irregular line joining Amsterdam, Haarlem, Noordwijk, Haarzuilens and Hilversum. More flowers are to be found in Holland for its size than anywhere else in the world and although the tulip is the most famous, narcissus, daffodils and hyacinths are prominent others.

The world's greatest open-air flower show is the 65-acre Keukenhof ('Kitchen Garden') at Lisse, between Haarlem and Leiden, set on the sandy soil so important to bulb culture. The Keukenhof is open to the public from the end of March until the middle of May. 'Tulip time' at its best can be spread over any of these weeks, according to the north European weather. In the Keukenhof's greenhouses you can see about 700 different species of tulip in full bloom long before the outdoor blooms are massed in the surrounding fields.

One of the greatest disappointments that a visitor can experience in Holland is to see fields full of empty stalks because all the blooms have just had their heads chopped off. This is done to allow the development process to begin again, producing the biggest possible bulb before lifting. Once the bulbs are lifted, in June and July, they are processed — sometimes put into suspended animation — according to the climate, altitude and soil of the country to which they are going.

The tulip, which grew throughout Asia 2,000 years ago, arrived in the Netherlands by way of the Balkans in the middle of the sixteenth century. Within a century tulip mania gripped the country to such an extent that the government had to step in and legislate to prevent widespread economic chaos. Men would pay thousands of pounds for a bulb with which they might start a new strain, even trading their houses, or a ship or a business. Some speculators were ruined. The country's top merchants and great business houses involved themselves financially.

The plant did not arouse interest in the rest of the western world until a book in the nineteenth century made a tremendous impact. This was Alexandre Dumas' *The Black Tulip*.

Today flowers and bulbs account for a quarter of the total horticultural exports. Among the many nurseries is Europe's largest for cacti, at Reeuwijk. Several towns have flower markets. There are important auction centres also, the largest at Aalsmeer, about half an hour's drive from Amsterdam.

Aalsmeer appears to be little more than a canal and greenhouses. The soil in surrounding areas is particularly good for flower growing and market gardening, and it is within sight of Schiphol airport. Many auctioned lots go immediately to waiting international flights.

The public are admitted to the auction for a small fee. It begins at 6am and the best blooms are quickly sold. Bidding goes on while the cut flowers are wheeled on enormous trolleys past the auctioneer and within minutes the blooms are being loaded into vans. Every weekday morning for several hours there is a non-stop procession of colour, flowers and fragrance.

Combined with a visit to Aalsmeer the English tourist will learn that there is a great deal more to the use of willow wood than cricket bats. In a yard at Bovenkerk, near Amstelveen, in a small brick building signed 'Klompen Makerij', is Mr H. Ratterman, one of the few people still able to make by hand a pair of the wooden shoes used by the people working and walking for hours on the soft soil in the surrounding market gardens. Visitors can watch this fourth-generation shoemaker. His is a dying art, for machinery can turn out three pairs an hour to the hand maker's six or seven pairs a day.

The wood is willow and it must be worked wet and then allowed to dry — in summer in the sun, in winter next door, at the very obliging baker's. A hand-made oak model serves as the mould for the shoes, but wooden shoes for 'difficult' feet, with niches hollowed to allow ease for those painful joints, are all part of the bespoke service. Ask to see the man-size wooden shoes made for an exhibition by Mr Ratterman's grandfather 84 years ago. They look exactly like leather, with eyelet holes and soles etched out, but they are as light as a feather.

THE COUNTRY'S folklore and the scene (in the old sense of the word, not in terms of today's pop groups, which flourish as artistically and imaginatively among the young of Holland as anywhere in Europe) gets a little more self-conscious as the practical Dutch turn their attentions to the space age.

Perhaps the best that is left is in the costumes. Although they can be seen in great number in Volendam and Marken, they are less consciously worn for camera-toting tourists by many old people on the sands at Scheveningen and at Alkmaar's Friday morning cheese market or in Zeeland.

Huizen and Spakenburg, east of Amsterdam, are two old towns where the fishermen's costumes have hardly changed since the Middle Ages. Then there are the dark blue or black flower-embroidered skirts, red check scarves and silver caps with gold sidepieces of the ladies of Staphorst. But Staphorst in the province of Overijsel is mediaeval, resolutely un-attuned to the twentieth century, the village of headline-hitting 'sin' trials and kirk-and-no-newfangled-inventions-like-the-motorcar on Sundays. Staphorst is perhaps the only place where a camera can cause serious argument and folklore will linger for a long time yet.

A unique street symbol likely to go the way of the mammoth is the wonderful Dutch street organ. It would cost about £3,500 to make a new one these days and there are only four or five people left in the country who can programme the music for these organs, many of which weigh over a ton. They are gilded and painted in rainbow colours, adorned with mechanical figures, cherubs, bellringers, matelots, ballet dancers, circus performers. Only two or three families remain who can cut new music, restore old dolls and their working parts, replace pipes, rebuild plaster work and retouch old painted scenes of Kashmiri gardens or Arabian Nights splendour.

The bicycle is still Holland, even though increasing numbers of inhabitants get around in cars and on trains, city trams, boats, planes. In congested city traffic the onus is always on the car driver not to hit the cyclist: never, it seems to the distracted motorist, is the onus on the cyclist not to get in the way.

It is a brave tourist who would tackle New York or London on a bike, but not so Amsterdam, where you can hire one easily and cheaply. There are even organised cycle parties complete with a pedalling hostess to point out the sights. For good measure the Dutch provide a survival kit — sticking plaster, guide books, sugar for extra energy, and a small bottle of spirits.

Of the country's cuisine there are few dishes which might be termed national, apart from the raw herring, a great speciality. Dutch food is international and good; portions are usually large. A Dutch breakfast (*ontbijt*) of assorted breads, cheeses, egg, cold sliced meats, jams and often chocolate grains to spread on the bread is an excellent start to any day; in many superior hotels it is giving way to the meagre 'Continental' breakfast.

Finally the language. One leaves mention of it to the last because, difficult as it is, it scarcely creates a problem to visitors. The Dutch are probably Europe's most brilliant linguists, but congratulate them on this and they are apt to belittle their own achievements. "But our language is so impossible, why should anyone learn Dutch?"

On my first visit I stayed at a small pension in Rotterdam and there even a parrot spoke English. I have been fond of the Netherlands and the Dutch ever since.

Margaret Hides

It is hard to predict the exact time, between the end of March and early May, but when the first mild winds of spring sweep over the land the seemingly endless fields of tulips, narcissi and hyacinths will bloom. This is the time to make the journey north from Leiden, through Sassenheim, Lisse, Hillegom to Haarlem and even beyond. It becomes a route of incredible beauty, a symphony of colour unequalled anywhere in the world, as these tulip fields at Hillegom, in South Holland, show.

16

Windmills were not a Dutch invention, but a logical people and the very nature of the country have brought the windmill to perfection here. There is hardly a day in this flat land that is without a breath of air. Breezes were first harnessed to grind corn, then in the fifteenth century to drain land, later to saw wood and eventually to drive heavy industrial machinery.

But the Space Age has taken sad toll and now there are fewer than a thousand working mills, whereas 170 years ago, 9,000 working windmills, sails up, heads turned into the wind, threshed a tremendous message of silent power.

The Association for the Preservation of Windmills in the Netherlands have a full-time technical expert travelling the country advising on renewals and repairs, even getting lightning conductors installed on these highly inflammable old structures. The Association has saved a number of ancient examples from complete decay and alerted regional authorities into salvaging the best of a dwindling heritage before it is too late. Many are becoming private homes after careful conversion.

In Holland if a person does something stupid it is a Dutch joke to say they have been hit on the head by a windmill arm. Don Quixote, tilting at windmills, is the personification of imbecility in Dutch estimation.

Some mills have two doors, one on each side; one door is always free of the turning blades while the door on the danger side is kept locked. This mill is in South Holland.

18

The Damrak, at the heart of Amsterdam's busy shopping thoroughfares.

Interpreters to help the tourists shop are part of the service of most big department stores. So, too, in some of the large shops is a playroom, where a trained nurse looks after toddlers while mother takes time choosing that new outfit.

Coffee clubs where regular customers rendezvous, beautiful window displays, shops filled with delightful things — all go to make shopping in the capital a pleasure (once you've found somewhere to park the car).

And for those wish-you-were-here picture postcards, many city trams have a postbox on the back. It is not unusual to see an Amsterdammer chasing a tram down the Damrak to post a letter.

Amsterdam has some 40 canals, mostly dating from the Seventeenth Century.

When the old city could no longer contain its steadily mounting population the town planners of the day constructed broad waterways in ever-widening concentric half circles. One 'spoke' of this wheel is the Brouwersgracht, or Brewers canal. Todays river traffic includes pleasure boats as well as working barges.

Moored in front of these tall, narrow warehouses of the Brouwersgracht are some of the hundreds of houseboats which provide accommodation for a sizeable proportion of the city's population of just over a million people.

The canals of Amsterdam, apart from the ancient ones designed as fortifications, were made for the transportation of goods; hence their sides had vertical walls for easier loading and unloading. Surplus soil from the excavated canals was used for the foundations of the houses and storehouses which the merchants built along the banks. This ancient bridge is on the Groenburgwal.

No other country has such an extended network of canals. Throughout the Netherlands well over 1,000 miles are navigable for ships of 1,000 ton displacement. Industry is located along many canals, which keep transportation costs comparatively low.

Forming the south-western edge of the old city of Amsterdam is the Oude Schans, which runs between the Amstel and the Oosterdok.

Northern Dutch cities evolved naturally along waterways. At first canals were useful fortifications. Later they became purely a means of transport and aids to fishing.

These waterways dictated a very definite, restrictive pattern, which is still clearly visible in the core of many Dutch towns: city walls, parallel canals, streets and squares joined by cross-linking canals, market place, a great church, town hall and fine houses all built upwards because the canals stood in the way of their spreading on the ground.

As engineering knowledge increased sufficient areas were reclaimed for whole towns to stand with their backs to the sea. They spread fan-shaped from the point picked for the harbour. Amsterdam is a perfect example of this. Its fan-shaped layout interwoven with canals is highly confusing for newcomers.

The special markets of Amsterdam are one of its gayest features. Here on Singel, near the Muntplein, is the weekday flower market, where blooms are sold from both boats and stalls.

The stamp market, which is held on Wednesday and Saturday, is on NZ Voorburgwal; and Amsterdam's flea market each weekday on Waterlooplein — an area of the city which during pre-war days was the thriving Jewish quarter, containing some important buildings including the Seventeenth Century Portuguese synagogue.

The book market, yet another of the interesting corners for those who like to linger in search of a bargain, is on Oudemanhuissteeg, close to the University, every Wednesday and Saturday afternoon.

The junction of Keizersgracht and Reguliersgracht in Amsterdam.

The characteristic colour of the old houses, shading from dark brown to subdued red, happens because Dutch brick was made from a mixture of peat and clay, and the mortar was sea-shell lime and sand. The houses stood protected under a thick tile roof.

The Dutch are a houseproud nation. Well cared for furniture and a riot of potted plants are features of most homes. And whether it is a Seventeenth Century patrician mansion or a house on a modern estate with the enormous windows so beloved by the Dutch, curtains are hardly ever drawn.

Following pages:

The Royal Palace is on The Dam, where the original houses of Amsterdam's fishermen once stood.

For over two centuries the Palace was the Town Hall. Built by a renowned Dutch architect, Jacob van Campen, its first wooden pile was driven deep into the swampy land on January 20th, 1648. It was completed in 1662 and stands on 13,659 piles.

The interior is a fine example of Dutch art. Well known painters such as Ferdinand Bol and Govert Flinck cooperated in beautifying the building. Allegoric ceiling paintings were made by Van Helt Stocade. The Burgerzaal (Civic Hall) contains a wealth of sculptures. In addition there is the City Council or Moses Hall and the famous Tribunal with a large number of Quellijn statuary.

When the building was finished it was the largest non-ecclesiastical building in Europe. In 1808 Louis Napoleon made it his royal palace while serving his brother as King of the Lowlands, and the city got a rather more moderate Town Hall. On Louis' departure his precious Empire furniture stayed behind.

Queen Juliana uses the Palace only once or twice a year for official occasions.

Enkhuizen, in North Holland, was once a wealthy trading port on the Zuider Zee. Its vast herring fleet has gone, its commercial importance has waned, but it retains a wealth of charm and interest, particularly along the canals and Westerstraat — the main street with its old houses.

The Drommedaris Tower, seen here on the harbour, adjoins the Zuider Zee museum. It was built in 1540 as an integral part of the town fortifications, and has dungeons and a beautiful carillon. There is also another carillon of note in the town, the 43 bells of the Fifteenth Century Zuiderkerk. From the tower of the Zuiderkerk a superb view across the Ijsselmeer rewards anyone willing to tackle the climb.

The old Mint is now a hotel. The Seventeenth Century Town Hall has become a museum and contains some Gobelin tapestries and paintings by Paul Potter.

De Zaanse Schans, a reconstructed village on the river Zaan in the typical *polder* landscape of North Holland, to be found a few miles north of Amsterdam.

At Zaanse Schans there are numerous windmills, each one different, a restaurant furnished in ancient Dutch style, a village street, old bow-fronted shops, and original green wooden houses which were characteristic of the Zaan district in the Seventeenth and Eighteenth Centuries.

The river scene is of constant interest, with almost non-stop movement of working boats on the river Zaan.

Alkmaar's Friday morning cheese market attracts visitors from far and wide to North Holland. Interest centres round the colourful scene in front of the Weigh House where cheese porters, in traditional white trousers, white shirts and beribboned straw hats — looking like something out of *HMS Pinafore* — hurry to and fro at a brisk jogtrot, carrying mounds of cheeses on the rocker-shaped board which is slung between the shoulders of two porters.

From mid-May to the end of August, the months in which to see the market in operation, the 'Cheese Express' races through the countryside from Amsterdam's Central Station, stopping to pick up visitors from towns en route.

Cheese is an important export, although of the many different varieties only Gouda and Edam are well-known abroad.

A sizeable part of the country's economy comes from dairy goods. Farming is of necessity on a limited-acreage, intensely-high yield basis. The average dairy farm supports only about 25 cows, but the milk yield is the highest per animal in the world, with renowned breeds such as Friesian-Holsteyn among the herds.

Reclaimed land is often extremely fertile. Some 58 per cent of arable land is used for cereals, 15 per cent for potatoes, and 7 per cent for sugar beet. Over a quarter of a million farms employ about 9 per cent of the population.

Slopes are not essential for winter sports. When canals and *polderland* are in the grip of winter you can be certain that somebody will get some pleasure from the cold and snow and ice — like these children of Schermerhorn, in North Holland.

40

A corner of the twin fishing villages of Bunschoten-Spakenburg, where the women-folk wear one of the most charming traditional costumes to be found in the whole of the Netherlands.

De Zaanse Schans in North Holland, a corner
44 of restored old Holland in winter time.

The Keukenhof — the 'kitchen garden' — at Lisse, in South Holland. The 62 acres encircling a Seventeenth Century country mansion display Europe's most famous spring flower exhibition, open from March until mid-May. Its pathways, streams, lawns, lakes and woodland glens are ablaze with millions of different blooms and heady with perfume.

On fine weekends you shuffle round in an endless crush of sightseers, but there are quieter times in the week when you might believe the whole 'kitchen garden' had been planted for your exclusive delight.

If one had to choose to see just one place to represent Holland at her most picturesque, it would be Delft.

In atmosphere and character a Seventeenth Century town, its canals are framed by linden trees which hang low over high arched bridges. Step-gabled houses with colourful window boxes are everywhere. The Gothic spire of the Fifteenth Century Nieuwe Kerk soars 357 ft over the heart of the town's market place. Craftsmen of De Porceleyne Fles factory jelously guard age-old colour and design secrets which have made Delft pottery world famous, although tourists are welcome to visit the factory.

Delft is not without an important stake in the future too. Dutch engineers come here to study at the outstanding technical college where they get sound and detailed training in land reclamation and hydraulic science — that lifeblood of Holland's survival.

The Town Hall in the Market Square of Delft, city of the famous Dutch painters Vermeer and de Hoogh.

Other great landmarks of Delft are the Nieuwe Kerk, which contains the tombs of the rulers of the House of Orange; the Prinsenhof, once the home of William the Silent and scene of his assassination which has now become an enchanting museum; and the Thirteenth Century Oude Kerk with its leaning tower, where the tomb of Admiral van Tromp bears unsusual sculptures recalling his battles with the English.

Delft, in South Holland, is host to the International Antiques Fair each June, and an annual Military Tattoo at the end of August.

The Fifteenth Century Gothic style Town Hall still plays an important civic role in the everyday life of the busy market town of Gouda, in South Holland. If you go there, watch the beautiful mechanical clock as it strikes, and visit the Thirteenth Century church of St John three minutes walk away. The church's wonderful stained glass and the superb economy of its architectural line should bring a momentary interlude of tranquility into any tiring tourist schedule.

Dordrecht, oldest city in the Province of South Holland, and meeting place of important waterways. For centuries this inland harbour city has been a thriving centre for trade. The richness of more than 600 surviving old buildings with impressive facades are some of the outward signs of its stature. So too is the Grote Kerk, a late Gothic cruciform church, which has been a Protestant place of worship since 1572. The church's impressive interior, with its colonnades, Gothic arches, star-vaulted choir and triumphal arch, attracts thousands of visitors. The stained glass windows depict scenes from the city's history.

But not all the enjoyment of Dordrecht is for those with an interest in history. It has gained great popularity with winter sports enthusiasts, and several important regattas are held here each summer.

St Cathryn's church, Brielle. 'In them hath
56 he set a tabernacle for the sun . . .' *(Psalm 19)*.

Rotterdam has progressed from fishing village to herring town and major commercial centre, the second city of Holland — all between the Thirteenth Century and Holland's Golden Age.

On May 14th, 1940 Rotterdam was wiped out by bombs. Today only the complete newness of almost everything betrays much of this story. The best way to get a graphic impression is to take the lifts to the viewing platforms, or the restaurant, on top of the 383 ft Euromast. The city and its modern road network spreads below you, so too does the unending seagoing procession of long Rhine barges, liners, freighters, tugs and transporters.

Then take the 'Spido' boat trip round the harbour. It starts from Willemsplein and lasts 1¼ hours. No port in the world has more to show, and to attempt its full story is to plunge into astonishing facts and figures of tonnages, refineries, engineering feats, pipelines and container traffic.

Rotterdam is now the hub of Europe's oil industry. Visionary plans for the harbour and the city's river links with the open sea began seventy years ago, and within the last twenty-five years brilliant assessment of the changing consumer needs of Europe and astute gauging of new types of cargo and container packaging have made it a global port serving the demands of the space age.

For green *polders,* Delft blue, fat yellow Gouda cheese, and 21 windmills all in a row explore the Rhine and Meuse deltas. On Saturdays in the summer, at Kinderdijk in South Holland, those 21 windmills will be turning. When this forest of water pumping mills gets going the wind-whistling whoosh of their blades is something no one forgets.

60

Winter snow fills the land with a new kind of light – the Doornenburg country house on the river Vecht, near Utrecht.

A Fourteenth Century watergate at
64   Amersfoort, in eastern Holland.

Dussen Castle is in North Brabant, the province extending between the Belgium frontier and the great rivers which cut across the Netherlands from east to west. The province marks the cultural-historical dividing line between the Catholic south of the Netherlands and the Protestant north — a religious division which holds no terrors, for it is a Dutch joke that in their country even the Catholics are Calvinist.

Brabant has the most beautiful mediaeval churches in the Netherlands. It also has scenery to comfort the eye and delight the senses: woods, sandy heaths which arc round tree fringed lakes providing favoured camping spots. Here much of the country's asparagus and strawberries grow. But Brabant is not exclusively rural; its major city is Eindhoven, the country's industrial heart.

Kerkrade, Oud Ehrenstein, whose museum contains an interesting collection of prehistoric, Roman and mediaeval finds from this corner of South Limburg, a part of the country with a culture going back 2000 years. There is no reclaimed land here; town names have Latin roots.

No hint either in this peaceful setting that Kerkrade is in the most densely populated part of Europe. The immediate surroundings were at the heart of an important coal mining industry which has been phased out only recently by Holland's increasing use of its big resources of natural gas.

Sociologists come now to this area to research how the Dutch tackled the latter day problems of redeployment on apparently model lines.

Kasteel Genhoes, Oud Valkenburg, is within easy reach of the charming town of Valkenburg, one of the country's largest inland summer resorts.

This Fourteenth Century castle in Limburg, with its superbly austere Fourth Century tower, houses the paintings of William Halewijn, a Dutch contemporary artist whose astonishingly moving interpretations of scenes and people from the Far and Near East have left a memorable impact when exhibited in Paris, London, Rome and Vienna.

These paintings are on show to visitors who can stay and enjoy a cup of coffee in the Roman cellars, or linger on the terrace absorbing the stillness of the beautiful Geul Valley. A momentary flash of iridescent orange and blue might pinpoint the spot where a kingfisher — or ice bird, as the Dutch call this most colourful of all the European birds — hunts along the castle's old moat.

70

Wijlre Castle lies in the valley of the River Geul, South Limburg, a province of castles and gentle hills. This is the Netherlands proper, 90 per cent Catholic, where an ancient dialect incomprehensible to Dutchmen outside the region is still spoken, and a northerner, whatever roots he puts down, is always likely to find himself referred to as 'the Hollander'.

Limburgians have a great capacity for gaiety, which comes as a surprise to people who instinctively regard the Dutch as stolid. Carnival time in the south goes on for days at Easter and Whitsuntide, attracting visitors from all over the country.

A few miles from Wijlre, at Vaals, there is a high forest meeting point between the Netherlands and her neighbours. It has become a favourite picnic spot. Families sit round the stone which marks the Netherlands on one side, Germany on another and Belgium on the third side. Children love the fun of having mother in the Netherlands passing the sandwiches to father in Germany, who passes the drinks to them in Belgium.

The ancient well, the statue of St Servace its patron saint, and the gay pavement cafes, epitomise the way the age-old city of Maastricht has a foot in more than one camp. So too do those tall TV aerials, which home into channels in neighbouring Germany and Belgium, giving many Dutch an unrivalled choice of viewing while allowing the local schoolchildren chance to master languages without tears.

Maastricht, provincial capital of the south and oldest city in the country, used to be among the strongest and most feared fortress cities in Europe. Its architectural splendours have Roman, Gothic, and Renaissance roots which owe everything to that history of the Netherlands going back far beyond the Golden Age of the Seventeenth Century.

Each street in the inner town looks out upon a church steeple. In greater Maastricht nine castles are to be seen, and no fewer than 1,450 monuments.

Lovers of art and architecture will find it hard to turn aside from the twin churches of St Servace and St John and from the Eleventh Century Church of Our Lady with their private treasure rooms, or from the old bastions and ancient gateways and the busy squares, tucked-away alleys and narrow shopping streets.

But Maastricht caters for all tastes. Much of the architecture of the city's apartment blocks and modern housing suburbs seems to owe more to nearby Belgium. Market day brings throngs from over the borders. Adjacent posters may well advertise performances by the city's famous male voice choir, carillon concerts — and a record-breaking blue film showing for its 45th week.

St Pietersberg Hill on the fringe of town is a great geological and biological curiosity which tourists may visit. Another face of Maastricht is mirrored in the river Maas, which runs through the city's heart.

The Begijnhof, a tranquil corner of Breda in North Brabant. Here was signed in 1667 the peace treaty between the Dutch and the British by which the Dutch surrendered New Amsterdam, later to become New York.

Hoorn Harbour in North Holland. Significant as far back as the Fourteenth Century, it became even more important and grew mightily prosperous when Holland's great fleets of the Seventeenth Century brought silks and spices from the East, cocoa from South America, and wood from the forests of Scandinavia to the quaysides.

In the Eighteenth Century it silted up, and the once flourishing seaport now sits on the edge of reclaimed land, one of the so-called 'dead cities' on the former Zuider Zee. But the beauty of its expensive mansions, gateways, and storehouses is not diminished. Hoorn is one of the joys of Holland.

The town of Hoorn, full of shadows from the past, is now a veritable open-air museum preserving all that is most striking in Seventeenth Century Dutch architecture.

There is Grote Ooststraat (the main street), with its exceptionally fine houses. Other notable buildings include the Sixteenth Century Hoofdtoren in the harbour, which became the offices of the town's whaling fleet; the West Frisian museum (1632); and the Weigh House (1609). Hoorn's principal churches go back to the beginning of the Fifteenth Century. The founder of the former Dutch East Indies, Jan Pieterszoon Coen, was born here.

Hoorn's open-air market still attracts visitors and people from the surrounding villages. The stalls with gaily coloured awnings offer a variety of local produce, which includes those wooden shoes · still widely used in north Holland by workers in the flower growing areas, who find clogs easier to walk in on the loamy *polder* soil.

'The shipmasters and fishers of Veere must make room in the harbour for a Scotsman if need be'. . .

This decree in the town's archives dates from the days when Veere was the chief port for trade between the Netherlands and Scotland. Two of the picturesque dwellings overlooking Veere's harbour are still known as the Scotch houses.

No one expects that the modern Scotsman will insist on his rights, but if he were a yachtsman he might find Veere's charming harbour so crowded in high summer with an international collection of boats that he would be tempted to do so.

Veere, however, is not only for people who like messing about in boats. Its decline as a trading port has left a storehouse of Dutch architecture with jewels like the Town Hall, which dates from 1470. Whether you arrive by water or by road the little Zeeland town draws you in to explore its tree-shaded cobbled streets and its antique shops and craft shops.

It is difficult to believe that almost all this editice is new, rebuilt from its own rubble after 1945.

Middelburg, capital of Zeeland province, had always been a place of pilgrimage for lovers of the past when in the final days of World War II it suffered severe damage. There was so much to lose. In the Middle Ages the city rivalled Bruges as a prosperous wool centre, but fighting, shelling, bombing and the breaching of the Walcheren dikes left not only Middelburg with its precious Thirteenth and Fourteenth Century buildings in absolute ruin; the whole of Walcheren island was devestated.

The Dutch, determined to restore towns and buildings like Middelburg's Gothic town hall, to their former glory, plunged into what is now remembered as the The Second Battle. When original materials could not be re-used authentic copies were made with all the skill and care of the ancient craftsmen.

Thursday market day is a delightful time to be in town despite the crowds. Many older women in Zeeland still wear national costume as a matter of everyday custom and Middelburg manages somehow to achieve the apparently impossible by being a lovely new city which yet feels old and mellowed by time.

Visitors should see 'Miniature Walcheren' (open April-September). It is Walcheren's story scaled down to one twentieth of its life-size, even to thousands of mini-trees, buildings, moving barges, ships, trains and swing bridges. You suddenly become Gulliver in Lilliput.

Zeeland (which is to say 'Sea-land') is a province of mighty estuaries, sandy beaches, and unspoiled towns like Zierikzee.

Zeeland's greatest delights lie in its people still untouched by the main stream of tourism, and in its old towns and harbours rather than in its flat agricultural landscapes.

It used to be the almost exclusive preserve of the holidaymaker with a boat, but now bold feats of reclamation and astonishing bridges leaping several miles across water are chaining the Province to the mainland. The province has simultaneously gained much needed protection from the sea and, for previously by-passed towns like Zierikzee, a greater slice of the tourist cake, plus firmer links with the dynamic trading routes of North and South Holland.-

It is easy to forget the threat of any drastic Twentieth Century transformation the moment Zierikzee enfolds you inside its Sixteenth Century gateway. Explored on foot, it is a town of pastel colours where the best is reserved for those who move slowly enough to see the old craftsmanship and patterning in plaster, wood and glass, or those with time to sit and watch reflections in the water.

Kampen, with its 'dunces-cap' Koornmarktspoort, one of the remaining gateways of the early fortifications, is a Twelth Century town at the mouth of the River Ijssel.

It is still very much a working port, but displays several fine old churches, a Seventeenth Century tower which has a beautiful carillon, and Fifteenth Century town hall with a splendid interior.

The traveller with time to explore this part of the country should make the journey a few miles further north to Gilthoorn, a village where there are no roads, only waterways. You abandon a car and take to the punt, joining the canal traffic with the postman on his daily round, the doctor, the baker — even a cow on a flat-bottom boat on its way to fresh pastures. Fields end at the water's edge; every garden has its own landing stage. At harvest time haystacks appear to be standing right in the middle of canals. Gilthoorn is a uniquely pretty place, one of several in this corner of Overijssel.

Deventer, renowned for its ginger cake and carpets, stands on the banks of the river Ijssel. Its origins go as far back as the Eigth Century.

Deventer was among the most important Dutch trade and cultural centres in the Golden Age, but while it is now an industrial and manufacturing city it has retained genuine beauty.

Much of the Grote Kerk is Fourteenth Century. The Thirteenth Century Town Hall has a unique collection of ancient books and manuscripts.

Outside the Gothic Weigh House, now a museum of furniture and costume, there is a huge iron cauldron which was once used to boil alive a Fourteenth Century forger.

An impressive mediaeval survival, the Fourteenth Century Doornenburg Castle stands in that fruit garden of the Netherlands where the rivers Waal and Rhine converge, an area steeped in history. Early European tribes, Roman legionaries, merchants of the Hanseatic League — and Twentieth Century armies — passed this way.

The imperial city of Nijmegen, beautifully sited nearby, leaps the centuries with its ruins of the Valkhof, Ninth Century court of Charlemagne, and the functionally modern Waal bridge which played a major role in the closing stages of the Second World War.

Much of this lovely region is known as the Betuwe. It is the largest fruit growing area in the country, a corner of quiet byways, small fishing streams and impressive relics of a bygone age.

The White Mill in Sonsbeek, Arnhem's municipal park which spreads unfenced to merge with the larger natural preserves of the Veluwe National Park and the Bergers Safari Park.

Sonsbeek holds many charms for the visitor. Another favourite corner is the view from a cave behind the Grand Waterfall, where you look out on to the park through a screen of tumbling water.

The park's highest point commands fine views across the Betuwe plain.

The old and the new exist happily side by side at Arnhem. Inside the ancient Sabelspoort gateway a predominantly modern aspect awaits you in the town centre.

Arnhem, equally popular with overseas visitors and regional shoppers, has a sunny ambience. There are excellent shops, artisitic fountains, attractive residential areas and wide tree-lined suburbs.

On the northern outskirts the 78-acre Open Air Museum provides one of the most interesting facets to any visit. Every Province is represented, showing something of Dutch popular culture and folklore. There are farmsteads, fishermen's cottages, typical Dutch interiors, old windmills, rural arts and crafts, costumes, old conveyances, even a complete village street. All the buildings, re-erected from their original sites, have been brought here to form a museum that is unique in western Europe.

St Eusebius church, one of several
historically important buildings which stand
on Arnhem's Market Square, adjoining the
98   Town Hall.

Springtime at Beesd, in Gelderland, on the Linge river.

According to statistics most Dutch people, if they had the choice, would choose to live in the park-like landscape of Gelderland, that Province in the centre of the country.

Forests rise from the Rhine valley to sandy tablelands, and 22 square miles are set aside as the Hooge Veluwe National Park.

When the flowers of spring and summer are gone, heather covers the vast heaths of Gelderland with a carpet of purple.

Uithuizermeeden de Menkemaborg, Groningen, is a country mansion restored and furnished in period style of the time when it was the private home of a Dutch nobleman.

The fertile north western Province of Groningen, with its woods, heaths and lakes, presents the characteristic Dutch landscape that measures up to many of the preconceived ideas of Holland. A network of canals threads its way through the flat land, coasting vessels thrust deep into the countryside, and some of the barns are as large as factories.

It is here you will find the stud farms and the gentlemen farmers. But Groningen has another face equally important; it covers enormous resources of natural gas, enough to satisfy the needs of the nation and bolster the country's revenues by supplying a large export quota.

Sloten is the smallest town with a canal in Friesland, the country's northerly Province sheltering behind mighty sea dikes, and rich in lakes, green meadows and dairy farms. Sloten's Eighteenth Century Town Hall has a small collection of antiquities, windmill and water gates.

In this part of the country, where summer is for sailors and winter is for skaters, the people have a language of their own and history which goes far back into Germanic times.

Man-made mounds in the marshlands of Friesland testify to very early primitive structures erected as protection against storms and water.

Museums, especially museums of the sea, are part of many of the towns, but the provincial capital, Leeuwarden, chose to be different and indicate the vital importance of farming to the region. The registered cattle breeders association has erected a life-size statue of a cow in the centre of town. Leeuwarden perches beautifully on three hills built out of reclaimed land. It has some very early architecture and parts of its bastions and old arched bridges remain.

There are eleven historic towns in the Province and, like Sloten and Leeuwarden, they all repay a visit. One which always has its share of tourists is Wieuwerd, where mummified bodies can be seen in the Seventeenth Century church crypt.

Harlingen, the ancient port of Friesland, is noted for its old gabled houses and its Hannema museum, which houses a fine collection of model ships.

The port stands at the edge of the Wadden Sea. From here boats ply one of the routes to the chain of the five small Wadden Islands, little known to foreign visitors. Mostly low-lying *polder*, they are blessed with quiet beaches and fine dunes. In late May and early June drifts of wild orchids cast purple shadows across meadowland.

The islands are on the migratory track between North Africa and the Arctic for some of Europe's rarest waders. In spring many of the birds pause to nest and rear their young in the Wadden Islands; in the autumn they rest briefly on their way back to the sun. At either time of year this corner of Friesland becomes a joy to ornithologists. And during high summer when the birds have flown, Dutch families move in for seaside holidays, going by boat from Harlingen.

Muiderslot, a Thirteenth Century stronghold with many historical associations at Muiden, a place of delightful interest.

In Muiden's colourful harbour you can often find fishing boats, pleasure craft and the Queen's yacht side-by-side.

Muiden lies off the Amsterdam-Utrecht highway. It is a gateway to Flevoland, that interesting part of the country where growing *polder* towns offer the discerning tourist a chance to understand what Holland is really all about — not the clogs-and-tulip image, but the hard determined slog of unrelenting reclamation.

108

The mood of the *polders* captured near Oud-Ade – the mood which imprints a memory of Holland that lingers indelibly in the mind long after total recall of other scenes and settings has slipped away.